# USC TROJANS

### BY CAMERON CLENDENING

Published by The Child's World®
1980 Lookout Drive • Mankato, MN 56003-1705
800-599-READ • www.childsworld.com

Copyright ©2022 by The Child's World®
All rights reserved. No part of this book may be reproduced or utilized in any form or by any means without written permission from the publisher.

Cover: Thurman James/CSM via ZUMA Wire/AP Images.
Interior: AP Images: Peter Read Miller 16; Danile Hulshizer 19. Dreamstime: Chon Kit Leong 4. Newscom: John Pyle/Icon SMI 6; John Cordes/Icon SMI 11, 12, 20; Matthew Visinsky/Icon Sportwire 15. Wikimedia: 7.

ISBN 9781503850392 (Reinforced Library Binding)
ISBN 9781503850668 (Portable Document Format)
ISBN 9781503851429 (Online Multi-user eBook)
LCCN: 2021930295

Printed in the United States of America

*USC Trojans celebrate another touchdown!*

# CONTENTS

Why We Love College Football 4

CHAPTER ONE
## Early Days 6

CHAPTER TWO
## Glory Years 9

CHAPTER THREE
## Best Year Ever! 10

CHAPTER FOUR
## USC Traditions 13

CHAPTER FIVE
## Meet the Mascot 14

CHAPTER SIX
## USC RBs and QBs 17

CHAPTER SEVEN
## Other USC Heroes 18

CHAPTER EIGHT
## Recent Superstars 21

Glossary 22
Find Out More 23
Index 24

## WHY WE LOVE COLLEGE FOOTBALL

Here comes fall—and here comes football! College football is one of America's most popular sports. Millions of fans follow their favorite teams. They wear school colors and hope for big wins.

*The Los Angeles Memorial Coliseum lights up for USC games.*

The University of Southern California is known as USC. The Los Angeles school's teams are the Trojans. They are one of college football's most famous teams. The Trojans have won 11 national championships. The beach is just 30 miles from USC's campus. But USC football is serious business!

CHAPTER ONE

# Early Days

USC began playing football in 1888. The school took a major step forward in 1905. That year, USC played Stanford for the first time. Stanford stomped the Trojans, 16–0. Soon, USC passed Stanford as the West Coast's best team. Stanford remains USC oldest **rival**. Their game is still a big one every year.

USC first became a national power in the 1920s and 1930s. They were led by coach Howard Jones from 1925 to 1940. The team won four national titles between 1928 and 1939.

**WHY TROJANS?**
USC was founded as a **Methodist** school. Its teams were first called the Fighting Methodists. That changed in 1912. Newspaper writer Owen Bird wrote that the team was "fighting like Trojans." USC has been the Trojans ever since!

# USC TROJANS

They came first! Here's the 1888 USC football team.

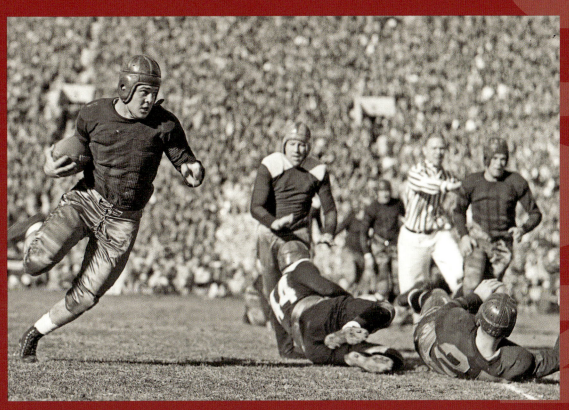

Homer Griffith helped USC beat Notre Dame in this 1932 game.
The Trojans also won the national championship that season.

CHAPTER TWO

# Glory Years

The Trojans were back on top of college football in the 1960s and 1970s. Coach John McKay led the way. USC won national championships in 1962, 1967, 1972 and 1974. After coach John Robinson took over, USC were champs again in 1978.

In the first **decade** of the 2000s, USC **dominated** college football. Coach Pete Carroll led USC to seven straight Pac-12 **Conference** titles. They also won four Rose Bowls and two Orange Bowls. In 2003 and 2004, USC was the national champ!

*← Left: Coach Pete Carroll brought the USC Trojans team back to the top in the 2000s.*

CHAPTER THREE

# Best Year Ever!

Fans think USC's best team played in 2004. Quarterback Matt Leinart was the star. He won the **Heisman Trophy**. That goes to college football's best player.

Leinart threw 28 touchdown passes. Running backs Reggie Bush and LenDale White pounded the ball on the ground. The Trojans scored more 38 points per game! USC was undefeated. They faced unbeaten Oklahoma in the Orange Bowl. The Trojans offense poured it on. USC won the game 55–19 and the national title!

**USC'S HEISMAN WINNERS**
Mike Garrett, 1965
O.J. Simpson, 1968
Charles White, 1979
Marcus Allen, 1981
Carson Palmer, 2002
Matt Leinart, 2004

*Right: Left-handed Matt Leinart stood tall as the USC QB in 2004.*

*The annual USC-UCLA game is always hard hitting!*

CHAPTER FOUR

# USC Traditions

Most schools have one big rival. USC has two!

One is right across town. The University of California–Los Angeles (UCLA) also plays in the Pac-12. The teams often battle for the conference title. They have faced off since 1929! Both schools' fans wait all year for this big game. Since 1942, the winning school has gotten to ring the Victory Bell trophy.

USC's other rival is Notre Dame. The Trojans first played the Fighting Irish in 1926. Many fans consider this college football's greatest rivalry. No other rivalry has included more national title or Heisman Trophy winners.

### FIGHT ON

USC's band is called the Spirit of Troy. It plays throughout each game. USC's famous song is "Fight On." Fans sing along. They hold up a "V for victory" signal as they sing.

CHAPTER FIVE

# Meet the Mascot

A USC student dresses as a Trojan **warrior**. He wears armor inspired by an ancient city called Troy. During games, this warrior rides a famous white horse. Called Traveler, the horse gallops down the track after USC scores. The warrior waves a gleaming sword as he rides! Traveler has been part of USC since 1961. Traveler has also performed in many Rose Bowl parades.

### THE COLISEUM
USC plays in the Los Angeles Memorial Coliseum. The stadium opened in 1923. The Coliseum was also host to the Summer Olympics in 1932 and 1984. A third L.A. Olympics is planned for 2028!

*Right: A horse named Traveler has been part of USC games since 1961. The 2020 horse was the eleventh Traveler!*

### CHAPTER SIX

# USC RBs and QBs

USC has had many great running backs. One school nickname is Tailback U. That's another name for the position. Between 1965 and 1981, four USC running backs won the Heisman Trophy. Mike Garrett was the first. Marcus Allen won the fourth. He was later an NFL Hall of Fame player.

In the 2000s, USC's offense focused more on passing. They were led by several great quarterbacks. In 2002, Carson Palmer won the Heisman. Matt Leinart won the award in 2004. In 2012, Matt Barkley set Pac-12 records for passing yards and touchdown passes.

> **FROM FIELD TO SCREEN**
>
> Many USC players have become famous in the NFL. One former player gained fame in the movies. Marion Morrison played in 1925 and 1926. He later became a famous actor with a new name—John Wayne!

CHAPTER SEVEN

# Other USC Heroes

USC's QBs have had great receivers in recent years. One was JuJu Smith-Schuster. He starred for the Trojans from 2014–16. Now he plays for the NFL's Pittsburgh Steelers.

**ON TO THE NFL**

No other school has had more players in the NFL Draft than USC's 510. Eighty players have been drafted in the first round (also the most).

On defense, USC **safeties** were the big stars. Ronnie Lott played safety at USC from 1977-80. Also a member of the **All-America** team, he went on to win four **Super Bowls** with the San Francisco 49ers. College football's defensive player of the year award is named for Lott. Troy Polamalu was an All-America for the Trojans in 2001 and 2002. He later led the Steelers defense and won the Super Bowl twice.

Many former USC players became sports **broadcasters**. They include Frank Gifford, Lynn Swann, Sean Salisbury, and Keyshawn Johnson.

*Troy Polamalu returns an interception for USC.*

CHAPTER EIGHT

# Recent Superstars

The tradition of great players has continued in recent seasons.

QB Sam Darnold starred at USC in 2016 and 2017. He led the Trojans to victory in the Rose Bowl and the Cotton Bowl. He then joined the New York Jets.

Running back Ronald Jones II played for USC from 2015-17. After his Trojan career, he helped the Tampa Bay Buccaneers reach the Super Bowl.

The newest great Trojan QB is Kedon Slovis. He got help in high school from coach Kurt Warner. Warner is in the NFL Hall of Fame! Slovis will lead the Trojans for a third season in 2021.

Who will be the next star to add to USC's great history?

*Left: In 2020, Kedon Slovis led USC to three wins that came in the games' final moments.*

# GLOSSARY

**All-America** (ALL uh-MAYR-ih-kuh) an honor given to the top players in college sports

**broadcasters** (BRAHD-kass-turz) people who describe sports action on TV or radio

**conference** (KON-fur-enss) a group of schools that play each other in sports

**decade** (DEK-ayd) a period of ten years

**dominated** (DOM-ih-nay-ted) clearly led or won over time

**Heisman Trophy** (HYZE-man TROH-fee) an award given each year to the best college football player

**Methodist** (METH-uh-dist) a form of Christian religion

**rival** (RYE-vul) a team that your school faces each year

**safeties** (SAYF-teez) defensive players who cover receivers

**Super Bowl** (SOO-pur BOHL) the NFL's annual championship game

**warrior** (WAR-ee-yur) a person who fights in battles

## FIND OUT MORE

### IN THE LIBRARY

Jacobs, Greg. *The Everything Kids' Football Book*. New York, NY: Adams Media, 2018.

Lowe, Alexander. *USC Trojans*. New York, NY: Weigl, 2020.

Sports Illustrated for Kids. *The Greatest Football Teams of All Time*. New York, NY: Sports Illustrated Kids, 2018.

### ON THE WEB

Visit our website for links about the
**USC Trojans**:
**childsworld.com/links**

Note to Parents, Teachers, and Librarians: We routinely verify our Web links to make sure they are safe and active sites. So encourage your readers to check them out!

## INDEX

Allen, Marcus 10, 17
Barkley, Matt 17
Bush, Reggie 10
Carroll, Pete 9
Darnold, Sam 21
Garrett, Mike 10, 17
Griffith, Homer 7
Heisman Trophy 10, 13, 17
Jones, Howard 9
Jones, Ronald II 21
Leinart, Matt 10, 17
Los Angeles Memorial Coliseum 4, 14
Lott, Ronnie 18
McKay, John 9
Notre Dame 7, 13
Oklahoma 10
Olympics 14
Orange Bowl 9, 10
Pac-12 Conference 9, 13, 17
Palmer, Carson 10, 17
Polamalu, Troy 18, 19
Robinson, John 9
Rose Bowl 9, 14, 21
Simpson, O.J. 10
Slovis, Kedon 21
Spirit of Troy 13
Stanford 6
Tampa Bay Buccaneers 21
Traveler 14
UCLA 13
Victory Bell 13
Warner, Kurt 21
Wayne, John 17
White, LenDale 10

## ABOUT THE AUTHOR

**Cameron Clendening** has written football books about USC and Notre Dame. A native of Dallas, Cameron is an accomplished football player himself, having earned co-Offensive MVP honors as a wide receiver during his senior year of high school.